VIA Folios 110

The Sleeping Gulf

Also by George Guida

Letters from Suburbia: A Novel

Low Italian: Poems

New York and Other Lovers: Poems

The Peasant and the Pen:
Men, Enterprise and the Recovery of Culture in Italian American Narrative

The Pope Play

The Pope Stories and Other Tales of Troubled Times

Pugilistic: Poems

Spectacles of Themselves:
Essays in Italian American Popular Culture and Literature

The Sleeping Gulf

Poems

George Guida

BORDIGHERA PRESS

Library of Congress Control Number: 2015937926

Printed in the United States.

Published by
BORDIGHERA PRESS
John D. Calandra Italian American Institute
25 West 43rd Street, 17th Floor
New York, NY 10036

VIA FOLIOS 110
ISBN 978-1-59954-088-7

ACKNOWLEDGEMENTS

Earlier versions of some of these poems appear in the following journals and anthologies: *Avanti Popolo!: Italian American Writers Sail Beyond Columbus, Blackheart Magazine, The Brownstone Poets' Anthology, First Literary Review —East, Florida English, Harpur Palate, The Italian American Writers' Blog, Italian Americana, The Long Island Quarterly, The Toucan,* and *VIA.*

Thanks to Anthony Julian Tamburri, Fred Gardaphè, and Paolo Giordano of Bordighera Press, for their continuing faith in my work. Thanks also to the many loved ones, friends and fellow writers who have inspired it. And thanks to Chris Cesare for his spot-on cover art.

For My Families

TABLE OF CONTENTS

The Sleeping Gulf

I.

The National Association of Peasants (NAP) President's Message

They stayed put so we're still there,
still doing all they did:
turning earth, plucking blighted leaves
from vines, pulling chickens from pots,
building fieldstone hovels to share
with beasts and ten children,
who work by our sides, learning
to thresh wheat, tan hides, herd goats,
raise barns, set snares for foxes,
pay tribute to kings and priests.

If we differ, it's in hearing voices
from afar, explain our choices.
We ignore them like masters of old
and call a summit on a small farm
near this year's lodging with a view
of the hills and coupons for espresso
at the local cafe. So please renew
in time for the cardoon harvest
and Feast of Saint Penelope.
Now, friends, is the time to believe.

Immigrant Rain

Siena

Easter rises, slaughtering
the ovine city. The tomb
tiles of this gelid room shine.
Hand-washed garments hang
on twine across space like fear.
The window's dingy shade
droops like a rheumy eye.

A trickle of water ignites
the empty hall with thirst.
Absent sounds of girls at coffee
visit the mind like succubi.
Boys of an intelligible tongue
have gone to resurrections
with kindly natives, as the lettered
run in pangs to paper and ink.
Outside the rain draws hostile blinds
and primes strange streets for blood.

All the lives in photographs—
sisters and brides to be—
dress for the advent of killing time.
On the bare desk a certificate of birth
lies open like an endless tale:
Natalia Verde, nato novecento sei,
Provincia d'Avellino...
Italian and English fill the room,
echo, fall dead apart.

I will pass this paschal day alone
in a foreign home, hard by
rain-washed alleys and open doors.
Inside, old men will stand
elbow to elbow at the bar,
old women like ceaseless aunts
will wreathe the table
and wave for me to enter
until the rain decides.

From an Airport Taxi

La Paz

The five a. m. lights are the eyes of a stray
sniffing El Alto's rubble for thresholds' scraps.
La Paz's crater, a cholita's fire
as she treads the dawn for bread
and scales the dusk in Paceños' dreams.

Paz and luz stand close enough to strafe like calloused feet
on dusty cobblestones treacherous as rainless months
beneath the grace of snow-capped Illimani
branded by the sun's vows into constellations' skin.

The dogs trot wild past shuttered market stalls,
past brick bunkers' graffiti. The cholita tightropes
the canyon's thin elbows, a week's bounty bound
in a blanket's folds on her river-scarred back.

The flowers, alive since fire's first breath,
since shamans pre-named the Southern Cross,
sleep in cold night's buds. The city was once
a map's music's gift, Pacha Mama's half-secret seat,
San Francisco of the altiplano,

where empire's echoes and beef heart grills
colored the streets all but sunrise.
The country's hollow name now holds the crater's edge
against landslides' death wish for empty feasts,
for lights' guidance of the lonely walker's way.

The Long Valley

Naples, New York

Mobile homes and appaloosa mares.
Everything's for sale in the valley.
In a fishing town Laundromat,
all the ways to sell ourselves
are posted on flyers with tear-off tabs.
One confuses the next.
Everything has a name in the valley.
Every name is a price.

When no one buys,
the flyers yellow, and appaloosas
roam the trailer parks. We roam
this Indian valley like the lost
pioneers we are. Down here,
the brown corn stalks of fallow
farms block out the sun,
stop dials and smother cell phones.

We don't believe this could all be
bought and sold, like dropping coins
into machines whose doors won't lock.
Someone will slip in to steal
the sheets we bought on sale.
Price means nothing, so we do
sixty-five on the two-lane route
from the edge of town, to feel in Gs

the curves and dips that seem to want
us here on earth. We didn't know
the valley ends with its mines
and tribe of hills, where the dead
main street is proof we paid
our way this far without a cause.
On the street an old folks' posse
shuffles to the firehouse

ice cream social. They've lived alone
in the valley's lifetime Saturday.
If only we'd known them when,
but then we'd be here too, forever
wishing long ago we'd learned
that money's no good, at least
for the things we need to see
the valley has no gentle end.

Union City, New Jersey

She says oh oh my daughter's moving
to New Jersey. I tell her
don't worry: Union City, New Jersey
is the new New York.
Oh oh she says
they have a fancy house with moldings
and no culture. I say that's just a myth.
The rich own the big city now,
the artists live as they should, on fringes
in the Union Cities of New Jerseys.
She says her daughter's neighbor Tony said
Yo, you gotta meet Carmine
across the street, scratching himself,
forgetting I'm Italian. She says I'm horrified
my daughter's a soccer mom.
No one here loves soccer yet, I say,
and if her daughter's kids do,
Tony can teach them all about it.

Move to Florida

Land of Good Living

Go. It's time.
The flamingoes
are real and waiting
for a pondside pat.

Go to marshmallow swamps
and soil yourself. I mean
oil yourself and lie
in the mango sun.

Let lagoons ring
your Northern Seminole war whoop.

Drag your intravenous cart
to the edge of Okeechobee
and shout, Miami's coming!
at the top of your iron lung.

Confess you believe that
St. Augustine is miniature
civil Mardi Gras with waves.

Take the grandkids
to the alligator farm.
Bring your rubber chickens.

Panhandle with mermaids
all the way to Tallahassee.

Smooch with a dolphin
a hundred miles from Kissimmee.

Forget the brown backyards
and frozen driveways.
Nostalgia dies
with absent heating bills.

Go. It's time.
The key to happiness lies
in the eyes of hurricanes.

Go. Have a Cuban.
Halve your weight.
Heave your cares overboard.

Water is good living.

Pluck a low-hanging orange.
The juice is good living.

Plant a Disney hickey on Minnie's neck.
Steal Mickey's cape, and take her
to Canaveral. Tattoo a rocket
on her thigh.

Break for spring,
and funnel your 401K.

Vote cracker with Latin kids.
Vote twice.
Fill in the swamp.

Stop at the Spanish church
next to the stucco strip mall,

and pray to the immigrants'
pink grapefruit god.

The Miracle of Stone Jesus and the Two Flamingos

Tampa

For when their beaks had been anointed with gold
and the tribal elders set them in the foremost yard
as upon a sacred mount, at the flanks of One
exalted and enameled to endure sub-tropic light
so whosoever should pass might look
upon the scene as upon divine assent
and in his passage kneel to pray,

then it was that I upon my journey
through this land of cinder blocks and sandy lots
did come to gaze upon the fowl adorned
in company of glazéd dolphins and El Señor,
that such study of binocular grace
did inspire me to make some offering
and please the One whose arms o'erspread
hibiscus shrubs as to proclaim, *This Our Father*
renders unto you, and so to myself bethought
to search for loaves and fishes, or fishes
at the least of all, and, with a heart so full
as I had never known, I flung pompanos
upon the walkway of cement, to manifest a faith
in Him who ever summons pastel beauty to His Side.

Then did arise such cacophony of tongues--
from the clipped frisking of Hispaniola
to the tempered patter of bygone Confederacy
to the pharisaical twitters of mockingbirds—

that from their entry doors emerged such denizens
in undershirts and sandals in the manner of our Lord,
betokening to this globe such growing discontent,
that mine eyes did see in theirs a sadness mute
as stone, for the putrid fruit of their idolatry.

Pendejo! Maricón! the multitude exclaimed.
That boy just ain't right! And when again I turned
to gaze upon the feathered harbingers, their aspects
like the Statue Shepherd's, were less beneficent
in shadows of the sun's descent, as though
flush of the flamingos and wrath of the humble
conspired in one malignant russet cloud
merely threatening to rain upon the keepers
and all they could imagine to possess.

Permanent Vacation

So let's to Maine
whose bears will roar our ears
deadly cute at six a. m.,
where wrapped in red fox
we will croon no more
the past to Corian countertops,
where December winds will freeze all thought
of perfect future, and white pine sap
will fix a grin like heroin.

Let narcotic green hilltops
kill our minds' hour.
Let every stone stream rise
just below the lips of our decline.
Let us forget directions to
the interstate of adolescent hope
we've followed up the coast so many times

with our now-dying mothers
who will never arrive.
Not recalling will save our lives
a thousand times, will our thousand lives
to sleep on forest needle beds,
safe from other predators.

We'll pulverize these bricks,
and let the red snow fall

on our cabin in the hills.
The river will bear it back to sea,
while we stand on the bank
and laugh ourselves stupid.

Flying to San Francisco

I have always been flying to San Francisco,
always waking after four hours' sleep,
swaying through the dawnlit terminal,
always leaving you behind.

I have always been thinking of you
as I stand in line with a boarding pass,
behind the foreign family laughing
from too much baggage and spare time.

In the row where we sat
I have always reclined my seat
just after the turbulence and sense
that I will get to San Francisco after all.

I have always been delayed,
stacked up over Oakland,
still east of where I need to be,
always out of your mind by then.

I have always been writing from Telegraph Hill
as I sit in traffic on the 101.
Even before you were born
I looked out for you over the bay.

I have always come here to contemplate
the Pacific current and cold

and the air that is always just right,
whether or not this city is ever you.

Cable Car Sonata

Nine-and-a-half miles per, whirr pincer gripped, how to stop unclear,
melody of the bell, brakeman from San Bruno. Ding.
Eighteen Sixty-Nine: The cart horse whinnies, sliding helpless backward
down California Street to a home in the New World dirt.

Expired terror in the masseuse's eyes, dragged down a Guoxii hill to the Geary-Ellis cross,
and down the block from the lucky Thai in waitress brocade haunts
the conductor's capped brain, barking like a wharf sea lion, but half the size,
three times the teeth. The sidle king of Hyde Street

clips tickets for the queens of Russian Hill. The dead pelt traders lie buried at his feet
near tossed pesetas and Indian scalps. You must chant, *The View Drew Some Who Slew*.
It Deeply Saddens Me. But the small wood windows are painted salmon,
and the floors are polished oak. The redwoods whisper *Golden Gate*.

One day soon the brakeman will leave his wife, strike out for Eureka.
His lever grip intimates. He fears the bridled Chinese youth deranged
by ceaseless dousing of curbs below his bunk will flash in mind
to mother's death by wok and father's cries from ox cart in the mist

and stop his throat for all that clanking history.

19

Green Barese

Bari

"On the 2nd of December 1943, the port was crowded with 30 Allied ships. One of these, the Liberty ship *John Harvey*, carried a secret load of 100 tons of mustard gas bombs, a precaution in case Hitler decided to invoke the use of chemical warfare. The seeds of the ensuing disaster were planted, merely waiting to germinate."

--Mackenzie J. Gregory

The Second Pearl Harbor.
What did he know?
then busy with a father
who had gone and come.
They were loading ships
the way they'd loaded him
the year the dust took hold.

He'd rather have gone to play
in Bambino Stadium. To him
Il Duce was never so grim.
Just look at the Germans
with their poison gas,
the American mustard ships,
the secrets he thought they knew
of the war about to end.

The raid shook the unclenched
fist the city was.
The flaming water tasted
of sailors' burning faces.

The drowning soldiers' dying
words confused him
but he smiled to think
they said Italians
could never end what they began.

At sunrise he searched the smoke
for his father's face, erased,
he imagined, by fate.
The Great Hand that loosed
the River Rapido again
had had its way. The cold sea
had taken enemies.
His father had willingly
died again for Bari's sins.

Toward home there were
the faces knowing
what the rumbles told.
His father liked to say
they had all come from slaves.
On Piazza Mercantile signs
he wiped sea-oiled hands.
At their hovel door his father
was a mask of American grins.
They would all be soldiers soon.

Camps

If my son should make it through,
he'll earn badges, place, geometry.

He'll meet those dead grandparents at the dock,
who'll spot the sad brown eyes and tremble with regret.

We'll mute the news, to keep him borderless,
from coyotes and their promises in killing sands.

My son's gaze evades patrols,
fixing on a fence to scale, as he's been trained to do.

His faith is the twitch of a prairie dog's nose.
The scoutmaster lures him with martial fingers.

We pull out our stash of yellowed maps,
pull up on screens the watermelon capital of Texas.

Construction's begun there on the Center for Guests,
where our son will sleep if he makes it through.

It's not the interned children who kill themselves
It's the mothers who have danced in dusty streets

as brides in gowns made of shrouded prayers.
The scouts' bonfire weds youth and death.

At his camp on the tranquil Sound my son has built
a pyre of ancestors' hails from moon and song.

He is the grounded eagle lit in orange and blue,
as foreign eyes assimilate the nightblown ash.

If my son should soar above a village square
where his thoughts are born in sabbath strangers' mouths

he would soon descend to the quarantined shore,
where his oaths would sound like shrieking at the city's edge.

If my son should make it through these hollow doors,
will he look behind for those hands and stars

beyond his tent? Or will he burn and rise
like smoke above the circle and, sovereign, ascend?

II.

I Pagliacci

"Death should not depress you,
death is natural," a young girl says.
Laugh at the grief that poisons your heart.

"Whenever I get blue
I go and shop for the perfect dress.
Death should not depress you."

I know she's not as smart
as the boy she's trying to impress.
Laugh at the grief that poisons your heart.

He'll miss the easy cue
to play his end, eyes glued to her breasts.
Death should not depress you.

"Tomorrow night I can do your chart,"
she says and sneezes. He says, "God bless."
Laugh at the grief that poisons your heart.

Clowns don't know when the comedy's through.
Everyone bleeds for a leading part.
Death should not depress you.
Laugh at the grief that poisons your heart.

The Sleeping Gulf

They look sixteen, the two dark girls from out of town.
The two light boys submerge themselves,
come up with shoulders bearing girls.

Pinching her nose, the first girl, not as pretty
but happier than her near twin, flips
from a broad back in perfect arc. *She got air*

the first boy yells, to say something that will make her feel
she's got him for their time here. She's got him
by the pool; at the ping-pong table; on the cabana chairs;

behind the dunes; in the shallows of the gulf; in a lobby corner
where after nine it's mostly dark. She's his discovery,
his night of wondering how to wear a shirt, lying

in a hotel bed alone, imagining her darker skin on his,
remembering her squeals as she leapt
into the balmy water like the nights

that launch themselves from youth the way
flares do and end as unseen smoke
in the sleeping gulf. She can do only things like smile

and smell like heaven. She can occupy the world
like a color. He wants to admit I am not enough
to keep you. I am someone else who will disappear

when my family goes away. You don't exist
without my brother and your cousin in the waves.
We are only currents that make the weather spin.

Soap Logic

Stavros dies at least three times.
Everyone wants him to go
and return a god.

We live to raise children
or we choose to live
in loft apartments where
our friends dress in black
like off-set actors.

You collapse in the playground
when your heart gives out
as you swing your toddler
back and forth. Your body
is whisked away.

Your spouse is left to forget.
I marry her in late July.
On Fridays we host soirees.
On Saturdays one of us dies.
The body is whisked away.

In the meantime we watch t. v.
and have trysts with Gina
and Deidre and Bradley and Ken.
Ken is stabbed in an alley
Stavros rises again.

We make sacrifices for art.
The next week one of us goes
to the doctor. The other one
dies. This time, as I lose
consciousness on the floor,

I spot under the couch
the keys I lost the day before.
All the stress they caused:
I worried for its effect. But now
I laugh and know no matter how
I go, I'll be back.

Without fear of consequence,
I stab Ken again (who's been back
for some time now) and think
of stabbing your former spouse,
when just in time you're back.

By now we are middle-aged.
(Yes, even in death.)
You are my friend again,
only this time our names rhyme.
We are forever and at once

personalities joined and split,
almost Siamese twins
married forever to a woman
and a part we have given
everything to forget.

Epithalamium

No, of course I love the smoked salmon
bridesmaids' gowns and celery centerpieces
on tables of ten it was as deeply satisfying to fill
with just the right members of family and friends
to prevent a scene over canapés
as to fall in love with you and your shy way
in the moonlight with nothing to be done.

Would I like to spend Friday night
going over the DJ's song list?
Do you even have to ask?
As long as we can download Madonna.

And let's talk again about limos.
The combo package sounds like
an offer we can't refuse, but
can we take some more time
to choose between black and white?

Finally, I must admit, I stay up nights
trying to imagine the best shoes
for the flower girl's dress and hoping
the best man will be gentle with me
and recite your mother some Yeats.

Morning Behaviors

The first wife woke at ten with imprints of sheet folds on dimples
like roads of summer colonies cartoon-drawn on tourist maps.

The second wife popped up at seven without alarm but with agenda
as long as cycles drowned in waves of visions and revisions.

The first husband lumbered to the bathroom and did not flush,
then slipped into the kitchen, to read a magazine he mocked.

The first husband yanked the sheet up to his stiffened neck.
He dropped to sleep again through keyboard clicks and hairspray spurts.

The first wife woke sometimes at nine, to catch the train to work.
In bra and panties she talked to the bed without response.

The second wife woke when school was out, and the child was calm
and the husband was willing to drape an arm and sing.

The first husband often slept past noon, to limn the day
with afterglow of wives recalling the distant planets and suns.

Wife Line

You are the bitter coffee.
I am the sweet lemon pie.
You are the new Mazerati.
I am the expired Percasette.
You are the calloused feet.
I am the side of the hill.
You are the three remote controls.
I am the green light, yield sign and full stop.

These are ways to compare
us to a summer's week.
This is my persuasive speech.
Here, my arm flailing.

Johnny was the boy who used his tongue.
Lester had a gadget for detecting coins.
Andrè drank warm beer and purred.

Before.
When.

Give me a five-dollar bill.
Put this leech on your neck.
Use the screwdriver
Leave my galoshes in the hall.

A cold child will kill you
in a darkened room.
Something like that.
Less bluesy, though.

Here's the recipe:
four cups flour
two eggs (with yolks)
tablespoon butter
pinch salt
three weeks cooking shows
bake at 275º until purple

Into the Blizzard

In the railway window I'll glide past places and wife left behind
for a new life on black ice, snow-dimmed view
of 4D, where I abandoned youth
and paths shrouded in powder.

I know it's never wise to bluff a night storm's charge,
away from near-new spouse and son, to welcome
a friend who's come to hawk his words, seduce a wife
he used to love but left for a late self.

The last forecast is a foot on the ground by dawn.
The city, as it so rarely does, should come to rest,
except for shadows on benighted avenues
we've spent half our lives parading lovers through.

In this weather I count on someone else to take me where
I think I need to go. From this green I see through flakes
the platform in the air, where I'll beg her pardon as if
she were the wind and the dead could care to forgive.

With More Art

You brought home pencil sketches
            of Dantesque dreamscapes,
       so I believed you loved art
       for art's sake, and I
put faith in shades, not in you.

The most vivid of these scenes
            is the pool of pitch
       swarmed over by Evilclaws
       and his winged demons
slicing the flayed and fallen
       so far because they
mistook the art of love for
            Dante's mortal sin.

You and I lived together
            in a savage wood
       where souls were gobbled, and
       where we might still wait
for a guide to lead us
       in contrapasso down
to punishments we've loved from
       when we conjured them.

Up for Steam

Uncle Albi in the basement
    with his weights worked up to it
        while his mother pushed and pushed
           all her children back inside
                the bedroom with all its dirty linen.

                Dirty linens mother ironed
          to make them smooth on faces.
      Italians like their linen crisp
    to keep things covered, sotto,
sotto sotto, sotta voce.

No one whispered the explosions
    inside their heads like insides
        of Easter lambs they slaughtered,
           swinging the hatchet down and down
              through blood-spurting necks.

                Dirtiest linens sopped up
          the Easter mess
        and the sacrificed son
      a rest from chopping
    down and down, in and in.
Mama kept it up, ironing, ironing.

Uncle Albi worked up to it,
      buying his mother the latest model
           filled and filled to make the steam
               when she let the button up,
                    enough for crisp sheets to hiss.

              Italian mothers always smooth it over,
          pouring steam through sheets.
    It rests and rests, sotto sotto,
until up again the button comes.

It doesn't take much,
      but always comes,
          sooner or later.
             What can you do?

             Uncle Albi worked it through
             before he did it.
          On the couch was where, because
    the bed still wet from steam
stunk like rotten animal.

The knife this time
      slowly and coldly
          without the passion of hatchet blows,
             but not gently across,
                deep, across, but not gently,

since, as he thought,
        she struggled with him
                on the couch
                        one last time, lying
                                with him
                                        on the couch,
                        pushed and pushed,
        dirtying the linen
he had lain there.

A real Italian,
his work done,
he pulled out
brush and iron,
filled it one last time,
read those words on the button
top and released.

III.

"The Magic of Olive Oil"

is chalked on the sidewalk board by a well-meaning clerk in the morning of her good cheer
and the promise of a day that may go as quickly as it wants, since so many lay
in store, in which her gourmet emporium chums become good stories
young enough to look good stripped, covered in olive oil, and sexed
against a back room wall, reclaiming aimlessness lost in ambition
for granite countertops and cast iron wall racks bearing decanters of it.

A lesser woman might have scrawled "The Beauty of Olive Oil" instead,
suggesting beauty is not what we'd hoped (half the oil's truth already lost
to machines on a farm far from Italy, run by a Fresno newlywed,
whose wife is pregnant again and God forbid this one should be autistic too.
If he split the scene, posed as an old-time actor, hair slicked back with you-know-what,
what magic would that be?), the bottles disappointing as Crisco in their virginity.

43

But this clerk's dreams are filled with groves and peasants singing on their way to a villa (The most romantic film she's seen) where from a balcony she watches labor and hears the car horns of Second Avenue. This board is her call to them. She has made a bowl of macaroni large enough for everyone: the pickers, the cabbies, the monks from up the hill and the business women coming home too late to cook. She is blessing them all, ringing them up to a cold-pressed deity.

My Father's Ink

His daughter's name in red across
his son-in-law's arm inspired it.
He daydreamed of all the women he knew
in the old neighborhood —
Carmella, Adele, Theresa, Joann —
of Mary, the one he married,
of his aunts and nonna, and of course
of his mother Antoinette.
But did he need American marks
to remember the goddesses
who govern life?

No. He asked the artist instead
for simpler pleasures, painted
for him and all to see.

They started with the first snack of the day.
On his right bicep a tray
of anisette biscotti;
on the back on his hand,
una tazzina d' espresso
with a piece of lemon rind
the color of the sun.

On the left arm they depicted
il pranzo: an antipast' of soprasatt'
and olives glistening with oil, then

macaroni with clams,
awash in blood-red gravy ,
sprinkled with cheese and pepperoncini,
primo piatto, the artist's finest hour.
Across his back, the secondo, a feast,
a line of eggplant rollatini,
aside a steaming heap of cioppino
with a small nest of radicchio
just above his buttocks.

Near the corner of his mouth,
for after he twists his fingers there
to signal satisfaction,
un bicchierino of grappa
for digestion and fellowship.
And beneath the second button of his shirt
for those times he wants to misbehave,
a massive sfugliadell'
every color of the rainbow.

With these images
he looks to himself
to satisfy any ooli.
With a simple muscle flex
he can order from his favorite places.
By baring a little skin
he can signify other Italians
of his age, era, region, neighborhood or block.

Should he be struck mute or
lose the use of his legs
to a terrible disease
his doctor has always warned would come

from eating too much muzzarell' and mascarpon'
he can still show people the good life
by opening himself to their eyes.

Italian American Hunger Strike

It lasted four hours
before a great uncle gave in,
dipping an almond biscotto
in his cup of chamomile tea.

Italian American Clue

: Gabriella, in the pasticceria, with the sfugliadell'.

: Antoinette, in the corporate library, with the master's degree.

: Vinny, at the detailing shop, with the chemi and the clay block.

: Joseph, on the trading floor, with the gold-plated pen.

: Maria, at the nail salon, with the Thursday special.

: Paul, in the regional office, with the actuarial table.

: Bobby B., at the tanning parlor, with the hot waxer.

: Sam, on the bench, with the gavel and the veiled threat.

: Joanne, at the latticini, with the scamorz'.

: Roseanna, at the Sons of Italy, with the genealogical chart.

: Sal, at the airport, with the one-way ticket to Sicily.

Mister Mozzarell'

No matter where you live
        or how your line advances
when vexing questions plague you
        Mister Mozzarell' has answers.

He's familiar with your family
        and doesn't like their chances
to succeed, but in their need
        Mister Mozzarell' has answers.

You've been told to shop the box stores
        where the products are predictable,
big as atomic clocks
        and mysterious as ritual.

You've been threatened with eviction
        for not having the full ransom.
You sleep in the room the sink's in,
        but Mister Mozzarell' has answers.

He remembers when the contests
        were won by the duke's best lancers.
Now that heroes are investors,
        Mister Mozzarell' has answers.

He's not living in the past
        or living off disasters
like governors with their bombast.
        Mister Mozzarell' just has answers.

If you want to find him now,
        no need to climb up in the rafters.
Mister Mozzarell's gone underground
        and taken all his answers.

Put your ear to the New World street
        where the Old World does its dances.
Then repeat what I repeat:
        "Mister Mozzarell' has answers."

And when he rises up to meet you,
        pretend you're worshipping Saint Francis,
for when your noodle's in the brodo
        Mister Mozzarell' has answers.

If You Want a Friend, Get an Italian

I could watch mine all day long.
He has the most interesting habits.
Sometimes he just sits in the corner and chatters.
Sometimes he jumps up and rattles the bars.
If I hum, he sings to me.
If I feed him olives, he spits the pits into perfect little mounds.

Saturdays he wakes up and immediately cleans his cage.
Sunday mornings he sleeps in, and stares at the t. v. when Mass is on.
On walks, if he sees another Italian coming towards him,
he gestures with his hands and makes funny faces.
He's very discreet about relieving himself.
He won't go out at all unless his hair is perfectly combed.

I could swear sometimes he's laughing at me.
Whenever the kids come home, he waves them over.
Sometimes he stays up all night, just waiting for them.
After he eats a big meal, he puts his hands behind his back
and strolls in circles for an hour.
Sometimes, for no reason at all, he starts crying and can't stop.

He's older now, but you still have to watch him around a female.
His hair is gray on the muzzle, but it makes him look distinguished.
He shivers a lot and smiles when I put him in the sun.
If I show him a map of Italy, he claps his hands, then sighs.
Sometimes he sounds like he can talk.
My wife is convinced he can say *Ti amo*.

San Gennaro's Head

San Gennaro's head is staring straight at me.
Why didn't you go to your uncle's service?
Why are you here at this feast?
What am I to you?

Saint Januarius, I say.
Christian martyr. Fellow Neopolitan.

Are you really Christian? Are you really Neopolitan?

I shrug. I plead, *My uncle's been dead a year.*
I visited him alive. I went to the funeral.

I know that. I'm a saint.
But the memorial's today.
The head rolls closer.
And how many will come when it's your time?
You think they'll save your blood in a vial?
You think millennia from now
they'll be lauding your sacrifice?
You think they'll cook all this sausage in your name?
Really, what kind of Christian are you?

I pause to think,
then gently roll the head away.

The best kind.
I never wanted to be a saint.

Goodfellas: The Poem

We gotta have calm now. State zit' and
get in the car. The other one
buys a Cadillac and this one buys a
twenty thousand-dollar
mink. That's a lot of money for a kid
like you. No more shines. I
never paid taxes. Never rat on your
friends. They're wearing it.

Remember, you might know who we are, but
we know who you are. Who
do you think you are, Frankie Valli or
some kind of big shot? He
shoots him in the foot. What do you call that?
The paw? The foot? The hoof.
A wing! I didn't mean to get blood on
your floor. Medium rare.

An aristocrat. He's a nut job. We
gotta toughen this kid
up. That cheap, cigarette-hijackin' Mick.
All day he's stirring a
pot of sauce. Chop him up. That's the flavor.
He kept fidgeting around.
The whole crew's gonna be looking for him.
Delicious. Delicious.

The man hasn't digested a decent
meal in six weeks. It's like
lead. Ba-boom. Put it on my tab. Happy
Chanukah! Smarten up.
Don't be a moron with the money. Do
what's right. It's all profit.
Don't give me the babe-in-the-woods routine.
Why don't you settle down?

She spends her life in a nightgown. She'll kill
him, but she won't divorce
him. That's what the FBI could never
understand. That's how fast
it takes for a guy to get whacked. Tia
Diavolo! The gun
goes off. Some kid gets killed. Friday
night was for the girlfriends.

Imagine that: a Jew broad prejudiced
against Italians. It's
poison in my eye. I don't know how to
make a restaurant. In
the oven you're gonna go, head first. In
Italian it sounds much
nicer. Louisiana u cazz'. It's
gonna be beautiful.

None of it seemed like crime. Nobody goes
to jail unless they want
to. Always keep your mouth shut. You may fold
under questioning. I don't
need this heat. Ya little prick, ya. You've got
to be one hundred per

cent Italian. Now I gotta turn my
back on ya. It's a sin.

Do me a favor. Don't paint any more
religious pictures. Don't
buy wigs that come off at the wrong time.
I'm aksin you for a
favor. I got things lined up. I got a
guy in here from Pittsburgh.
I was still very attracted to him.
Sammy Davis, Junior.

I just want to make sure I'm not kissin'
Nat King Cole. He's treatin'
me like I'm half a fag or somethin'. I
wish I was big just once.
If I even look at anyone else,
he'll kill me. I keep 'em
up all night. What he really loved to do
was steal. It's not even fair.

Security? It's a joke. You had to
have a sit down, or you'd
be the one who got whacked. But when I heard
all the noise, I knew they
were cops. You boys want some coffee? Give these
Irish hoodlums a drink. This
is from Mister Tony over there. It looks
like somebody we know.

For a second I thought I was dead. So
the wife says, *Shut up. You're
always talking.* And this one's sayin', *What*

do you want from me? You're
breakin' my balls? I'm kiddin' witchu. Like
I'm a clown: I'm here to
amuse you? Dance. Did you see my painting?
It's like the real people.

There must have been two dozen Peters and
Pauls at the wedding. I
had paper bags full of jewelry. Being
a gangster was better
than being President of the United
States. Nobody ever
tells you they're going to kill you. It was
better than Citibank.

We were wise guys, you varmint. You remember
that other guy, the one
they made the beef with? There was Jimmy and
Tommy and Anthony
Stabile and ... Maurice Valencia. Hey,
what's up, guy? He oughtta
wear a sign. He's hanging over my neck
like impending danger.

It was real greaseball shit. He gave me ten
grams of valium and
sent me home. He's a bad seed. What am I
supposed to do, shoot him?
As far back as I can remember, I
always wanted to be
a gangster. You automatically
make them out to be saints.

When they found Carbone in the meat truck, he
was frozen so stiff, it
took them two days to thaw him out for the
autopsy. I gotta
admit the truth. It turned me on. How could
I go back to school? As
soon as I got home, I started cooking.
We all know what it is.

It's my lucky hat. And that's that. Thirty-
two hundred dollars for
a lifetime of service. What do you have
me on the pay-no-mind
list? Pay me. I want my money. What am
I, a mirage? What am I,
a schmuck on wheels? I'm parking cadillacs.
What's the matter with you?

You're still bouncing around from girl to girl.
You don't feel like you're in
construction. Shitty jobs for bum paychecks.
We'll see how much of a
good guy you're gonna be then. You're a real
pisser. I thought you had
one of your bitches in here. Like I was
never nothing to you.

Hang up once more, and you're gonna deal with
me. You're making me think
what I did. You're gonna tell me somethin'
today, tough guy. No more
bullshit. My dream comes true. It's a Jewish
holiday. They won't find

out till Tuesday. Forget about it. I took
care of that thing for ya.

That Brooklyn thing? Down on the boulevard,
Rockaway Boulevard.
You gave 'em nothin', and they got nothin.'
Why did you do that? It's
a license to do anything. It's a
coupe. I love that car. Get
it outta here. I get to live the rest
of my life like a schnook.

Now go get your shinebox.

Sul serio

Use the good body God gave you.
Mai indietro.
Mai indiritto.
Mai indeciso.
Mai incognito.

Walk through your glorious palsy,
go zoppo, zoppicante,
in flagrante delicto.

Hammer the nails by hand
and one by one
mortar the stones
until the cathedral can stand,
until all the work that lasts
a thousand years is done.

Don't look down from the scaffold.
Sempre su!
Dai!
Forza!
Avanti!
Sempre fala new,
a thousand years new.

Wield your guild card as stiletto.
Punch holes in rector's walls

like bans on thought.
Per dire la verità
the stucco is alive
with roaches and rats, with
tutto quello che vive
dentro la mente. The walls
are crawling, as you crawl
unless you stand like a statue
and wave your chiseled flag.

Malaria

What illness? Bad air.
Verdant fog
skulks in the wings.
The stone village.
Aria. The costly stage.
You watch Verdi on t. v.
The balefaced tenor,
scurolescent soprano.
The boards between
marsh and office
pumped with faux.
In Verga's words,
nails you to a hovel door.
Your infant son inside.
A misdrawn breath.
Rheumatic digits.
Malingering eyes
maladied as grapes
on stricken vines
(phylloxera). Once prima
donna plump, taken once
to the Côte d'Azur.
Breezes and croupiers'
ill will. The disease
in retreat with the franc,
lira, peseta, drachma. You read
of distant peasant fields.

You walk with a limp.
Vice President
for the Western Hemisphere.
From your desk a view
of the brick-lined pond.

Italy and Everyone

I miss Italy and everyone there I don't know.
I'm not fooled by this amnesia.
I'm not gulled by wife and child.
I remember that stone path down the hill.
I remember the view from the cliff.
I still awaken to the ancient tower's bells.

I know sin can't be unlearned.
I knew both routes to the cathedral.
Italy never questioned my faith.
The ruins whispered counsel.
I whistled on the hilltop.
Italy never told me who I couldn't be.

The True Virtuoso Spirit

> "Few Italians have the true virtuoso spirit.
> For the most part their enthusiasm is adapted to
> suit the time and opportunity to practice imposture."
> —Edgar Allan Poe, "The Cask of Amontillado"

You may think to yourself, *In Italy art is everywhere,*
but in Italy don't say this aloud.
If one of them hears, he will join you in your joy,
and such a marriage cannot end well.

When you pass a tenth-century tower,
let flow the bowels, to throw them off the scent.
Ignore the busty, raven-haired seductress
shifting her weight at the gelateria.
Her eyes convince you to believe
she savors the nocciola thus.

The Carabinieri are merciless too,
with all their second-hand smoke.
Their directions to museums are rarely direct,
and their uniforms make you itch.

They all know you've been through before
in green and blue and red and white and gold,
marching on their capitals for souvenirs and charm,
as they slink in tears to ballot boxes
where they bury the musical name
of every Italian who's ever lived.

Your textbook talk will only court intrigue.
They will gather on benches and in narrow streets,
exchanging secrets they think you ought to know.
If you smile as a gesture of good will,

rest assured they will place you in their homes,
whistle a dramatic air, and stroll away.

Piccola Italia

When the last Italian-speaker dies,
we'll finally open our business,
the Vegas idea, resort casino-
culture spa, Piccola Italia.

Guests will arrive with coupons
we mass mail in October,
redeemable for lessons
in conjugating verbs,

since italianitá is a gamble,
that depends on living the tongue.
They'll have to learn at least: *Dov' é
la mia camera?* by check-in.

Campanile bells of Norman design
will clang them awake for espressi and
biscotti from a nonna's recipe
book published in Boston.

Called cittadini, they will
stroll Il Centro Storico
with actors trained on weeks of
Rai Uno news broadcasts.

On the way we'll force them to chat
with paesani re-enactors

in streets wide as Cinquecentos,
copied from a town outside Naples.

Many will apprentice to masons
at work on a flint cathedral
where the Bishop of Nevada
will bless a few pretend goomads.

One week in we'll simulate steerage.
Cittadini will walk to a dock
on our Atlantic lagoon, to sleep
with bedrolls and children we supply.

They'll spend three nights aboard
our steamer, *La Stella Meridionale*,
down in a hold filled with cow manure
treated to smell like humanity.

Off the boat they'll disperse, led by
padroni played by croupiers,
settle in hotel blocks arranged
by hilltop villages we assign.

After two more weeks of labor, when
they speak enough Italian to joke,
we'll help them, day by day, forget
inflections, declensions, idioms,

forget how to speak, how to find
the way on foot to aunts' houses
hand-built by carpenter uncles,
to leave St. Roc, pasticcerie,

so they have to remember
the culture now in their bones
until they earn enough chips
from work and the slots, to buy

the sprinklered lawns and hedges
that are their destiny.

IV.

Natural State

Twenty more bombs fell by noon
on a city where rubble makes it hard
to tell. The shrieking that could only be
the pierced, crushed, bloodied mother
with child toddling near the body
or the child charred to coal
and mother bent and gasping for air
without that scent failed to stir
the gray and gunless man at table
set in an alley by an open door,
who sipped from a clear bottle's stream,
with each sip sitting back to stare
into airborne dust that cloaked
a certain morning in the cedars' shade.
In the whistling of the missiles
he was smiling like a pardoned thief.

Today you turn up at my door
with a bottle of pinot noir
and stories of bars in L. A.,
Houston, Atlanta, Detroit.
I am full of cities just now,
filled with wonder for their life.
Your history of these places
is aging strippers and snippets of talk
about bands and their singers who died
with the promise of songs inside.

You will leave soon for a city club,
close to fifty, drink yourself
closer to what I see at first
as an early end, but then I'm with him,
that gray man in that city, that man
no older than you if you lived
with his dust and screaming sky,
and I pour a half a bottle for myself,
handing you the rest, and toast
the blessed onset of our natural state.

Who Killed Osama Bin Laden?

Yes, it could have been
the Philadelphia Phillies,
the way their fans are chanting,
U-S-A, U-S-A, U-S-A!

Or maybe my alcoholic neighbor
who was absent from his deck today.
He drives an S-U-V, S-U-V, S-U-V
and lately has been sober as an imam.

The motive is clear for
subway conductors living since 9/11
in fear unchecked by random
searches and passenger police.

As it is for the Arab boy born
in Brooklyn, sickened for life
by agents unmanning
his father on Flatbush Avenue.

My own boy is surely too young,
but my father is always suspect,
a crack shot from 500 yards
and rock-ribbed as they come.

But the joy is bipartisan,
so it could have been

the Peace Corps or all nine
Supreme Court Justices.

But wait, they're about to announce it
on CNN, IPad, cell, and homeland blog,
broadcast speeches and reviews
that will explain him finally away.

My Mother Shares Foreign Policy Insights

They're not freedom fighters, George. They're terrorists.
I don't know where you get your information.
If it quacks like a duck, you don't arm it with missiles.

The Chinese don't care either way, as long as they get their oil.
I laugh when people call them communists.

We should stick to our own hemisphere, focus on the Mexicans.
They're very hard working, and we know them.

With the Russians you never know what to think.
One minute they're invading; the next, they block your invasion.
They're always angry, because it's so cold.

Diplomacy's only worth the guns you put behind it.
Ask the British. Who was more brutal than them?
I'm glad you didn't marry that girl from London.

Don't get me started on the French.
The last reliable one was Lafayette.

The Germans are better since they got it out their system.
Believe me, you want them on your side.

And don't forget the Pakistanis. They have loose nukes
and don't like a whole subcontinent.

The problem is there's no more Red Coats.
Today, no one stands in front of you when they fight.
What we need is flexible strike capability.
That means we cut down on fighter planes.
It's the military industrial complex. Eisenhower.
You were probably daydreaming when they covered that in school.
History class is like a scuola past' for macaroni.
Sometimes you need to save a little water for the sauce.

Anyway, what we need the most is real ambassadors,
not the Governor of Arizona's niece or Shirley Temple.
Of course they cover up the breaches.
They lie when it's convenient, like your cousin Tony.
It's for the media.

You remember the James Bond movies your father likes to watch.
You can learn a lot from them.
Except about foreign aid.
Another story.

Emigdola

I'm standing there being a citizen, an American.
sliding my cart into another, to clear some space
and he revs his engine, revs it, like that, and zooms his truck
right past me into the spot. Zooms. An inch from my foot.

He passes the foot he almost crushes, and yells
out the window, *Really?* This guy is fifty-something
if he's a day. And I think, *Nice goin', Einstein.*
And I want to say what else I think. But knowing what I know
about psychology, I say, *You havin' a bad day, Bud?*

He doesn't even look at me, no eye contact,
and what does he say? He says, *Get a grip.*
Get a grip. Like I'm the one.
And it's an even older cliché. And I hate clichés.
And I hate him, want to hit him. So I don't get back

in my car. I wait for him to make a move.
They say you never know who has a gun.
But it's a rich town supermarket. Jackass in an S. U. V.
What's he gonna do? A gun? I'm in a leather coat.
For all he knows, I'm a gangster. I'm a thug

with a wife who needs cheese. I'm out here now
with this moron, and I can feel my heart. What's the word?
Adrenaline. Adrenaline rush. Like to hell with this
being a bad idea. Bad idea? My whole life's a bad idea.
So I want to take a step. Adrenaline. Step up to him.

Then I hear a dog bark. And I hear him lock his doors.
It's his dog in the front seat. Locked in. So I stop.
Not why you think. It's a toy poodle. Yap, yap, yap.
All I can hear. Yap, yap, yap. Like a barking rat.
And he takes the cart I left, to make space.

He leaves the dog, who's barking at me now.
Jackass starts walking. Walks right past me. Keeps walking.
Showing me his teeth. The dog. I hear myself yell.
Right past me, and I'm yelling at the dog.
Except now he's quiet, like I'm not even there.

To the Young Black Man in the ITALIA Sweatshirt

C'è Carlo, c'è Mauro, c'è Francesco, c'è Pietro, c'è Gianluca
e c'è Il Nero.
I'm ashamed to say it,
but that's what they'd say,
those fans in Italia,
watching Sunday calcio
on the couch for the pranzo head count.

You'd be the black one,
the one who counted less.
I'm not even sure they'd want you
to wear it, since they see themselves
as a people, though so many in one,
so dark, so down themselves so long,
they could copyright *soul*.

And would you really like their company?
They sing hundred year-old songs
about troubadours, walking
narrow streets where you greet everyone,
whether you mean it or not.
The team they cheer is lucky
if they score twice a game.
When they lose, the ragazzi don't go
to clubs, but retreat to their mothers
for five-course meals and stories
about foreigners ruining the city.

Why did you pay so much
for these colors?
when you could have sported CAMEROON,
for all the black ex-pats,
whose fathers know the peril
of taking a European side.
Isn't Brooklyn enough of a country for you?

I hope the cloak of the azurri warms,
at least until you shop again,
and through your bread wrap your body
in someone else's spirit and skin.

Jury Duty

The actor playing counsel
looks just like John Amos,
who in *Roots* was Kunta Kinte,
proud slave, and I too
want to flee and be free
to eat a morning snack,
sing along with the hanging
radio in my shower, towel off
and take a nap, wake up,
walk my dog and eat again:
the kind of freedom John Amos had
as James Senior on *Good Times*,
another show, another slavery.

No one here at least will explode,
passed as they are through metal
detectors and cops named Phil and Ed,
who tell the judge they think
everyone belongs in jail
like impaneled jurors,
like frescoed figures
on courtroom ceilings,
memorized again and again
by bailiffs, judges, lawyers, clerks,
all the actors we watch
in this new court house
built for public good

with private funds you can see
on big screens, in stadium seats,
few empty or occupied
by those in whose hands
your fate rests.

In the jury restroom a voice
piped in as I almost release
is narcotic, whispers a pledge
to make our stay here
comfortable as can be,
bondage reduced to the time
it takes to shackle someone else,
unless upon the auction block
you happen to appeal.

The Rich

We like their houses.

Requiem for Privacy

Leave him alone. He's crafting beer.
He's noodled a vat. He's hoarding hops.
He's rejiggered Bacchus's smile.
She's sewing a bonnet from Terpsichore's rinds.
She's distilled wafts of jasmine mist.
She's lassoed a lullaby in stitch.

Leave them alone. They're scoring balustrades
with pitchforks. Don't bother them.
They're at work. They have a foundry.
They've kept the neighborhood's fires underground.
They've been mopping the streets by night with their tongues.
They're cutting a downtown cornstalk maze.

For God's sake, keep your distance.
They're vacuuming the secret B & Bs.
Please respect the screaming crickets
they're coating in chocolate for sale
at the ranch-owners annual cactus stomp.
Invitations went out with the trash.

Let go of the towers you're holding.
They don't belong to you. Look up.
The Luckies are floating overhead.
They're juggling oil balloons.
Let the misses fall. You have time to run.
Demand your refund anywhere but here.

The Coach's Last Day

Look at me. Listen.
You were never any good.
I saw it right away.
The way you shuffled
and your eyes drifted nowhere.
What is it you lacked?
Not heart.
More heart and mind.
That's tough to accept.
So why am I saying this now?
Sure, I could just have cut you,
let you walk and guess why.
Then you're back to lying awake,
staring at the bedroom curtains
and I'm back to lying.

What else could you have done?
Nothing.
What are you in the sum of things?
(Don't take this personally.)
Nothing.
I am the Nothing that gets to tell you.
You're not good enough for this.
But don't let that stop you
from reaching for the stars.
Where are the stars?
In the middle of nothing.

So you can do it.
You just can't do it here.
Because we have a relationship
based on trust. Like a family.
We're a big family.
That's the philosophy I got
from my old neighborhood,
from my parents, gone now. Like you.
Like the kind of family we had
for a while, when it was us
against the world.

The truth is we were the world,
an idea you had to slap a uniform on
to see. But those colors are just a piece
of the rainbow. You are the rainbow.
All the colors together
or what's left
when you take them all away.

About the Author

GEORGE GUIDA is the author of eight books, including the collection of poems *Pugilistic* (WordTech Editions, 2015), and *Spectacles of Themselves: Essays in Italian American Popular Culture and Literature* (Bordighera Press, 2015). His poems have appeared in many journals and anthologies: *Alimentum, Barrow Street, Blackheart Magazine, Controlled Burn, Harpur Palate, Inkwell, Italian Americana, J Journal, Literary Bohemian, Literature and Gender, Rabbit Ears: An Anthology of T.V. Poems,* and *VIA,* among other journals and anthologies. He teaches English and creative writing at New York City College of Technology and Waldon University, and serves as Poetry Editor of *2 Bridges Review*.

Bordighera Press is an imprint of Bordighera, Incorporated, an independently owned not-for-profit scholarly organization that has no legal affiliation with the University of Central Florida or with The John D. Calandra Italian American Institute, Queens College/CUNY.

www.ingramcontent.com/pod-product-compliance
Lightning Source LLC
LaVergne TN
LVHW041302080426
835510LV00009B/848